PATRICK ROY

PATRICK ROY

Champion Goalie

Morgan Hughes

Lerner Publications Company • Minneapolis

In memory of my father, Bill, who started me on hockey so long ago, and for the kids, Gwyneth, Jack and Willa, for whom games such as these should always remain just games.

This book is available in two editions:
Library binding by Lerner Publications Company
Soft cover by First Avenue Editions
241 First Avenue North, Minneapolis, Minnesota 55401

Website address: www.lernerbooks.com

Hughes, Morgan, 1957–
    Patrick Roy, champion goalie / Morgan Hughes.
       p.   cm.
    Includes bibliographical references (p.) and index.
    Summary: A biography of the Colorado Avalanche's all-star
goaltender whose career achievements include winning three Stanley Cups.
    ISBN 0–8225–3660–9 (hardcover : alk. paper) — ISBN 0–8225–9813–2 (pbk. : alk. paper)
    1. Roy, Patrick, 1965– —Juvenile literature. 2. Hockey
goalkeepers—Canada—Biography—Juvenile literature. [1. Roy,
Patrick, 1965– . 2. Hockey players.; I. Title.
GV848.5.K67H84   1998
796.962'092—dc21
[B]   97–30587

Manufactured in the United States of America
1 2 3 4 5 6 – JR – 03 02 01 00 99 98

Contents

Rocky Mountain High

As a rule, the month of June isn't the best time of year to be in South Florida. The hot and steamy weather feels more like beach weather than hockey weather. But on a muggy June day, the Colorado Avalanche stormed into Miami Arena, determined to finish its business with the Florida Panthers. Leading three games to none in the National Hockey League's Stanley Cup Finals, the Avalanche was just one win away from winning the first championship in franchise history. For 16 years, the team had been based in Quebec City, Quebec, and called the Nordiques. In the summer of 1995, it had moved to Denver. The Avalanche was trying to become the first NHL team to win the Stanley Cup in its first year in a new city.

The team had an international cast of all-star players, including scoring ace Joe Sakic from western Canada, tough and talented Peter Forsberg from

Sweden, speedy Valeri Kamensky from the former Soviet Union, and rangy **defenseman** Uwe Krupp (YOO-ee KROOP) from Germany. No player was more keenly watched, however, than the masked man between the red pipes, goaltender Patrick Roy. The Avalanche owners had brought Patrick to Denver for one purpose: to lead the team to a championship.

Patrick is a French Canadian whose last name is pronounced "wah." Roy means "king" in French. Patrick, 6 feet and 192 pounds, had proven many times that he could carry his team to greatness. As he prepared for the game on this hot June day, he was calm and ready for the coming challenge. No amount of pressure or attention could knock him off his normal stride. Patrick followed the same routine that day that he had on other game days. After the morning practice, he went to the team's hotel for his pregame meal.

"I always eat a steak with mashed potatoes and peas," he says, "with a salad on the side. Then I take a nap around one o'clock. At three o'clock, I'll sit up in bed and try to imagine myself playing the game. I think about the players I'm going to play against, the things they might do, and ways I can stop them from scoring."

Stopping the opponent's scoring had been Patrick's challenge since 1985, when he entered the NHL and began playing with the Montreal Canadiens. On this hot Miami night, facing the Panthers, Patrick would have to be as close to perfect as he'd ever been.

Patrick stops a point-blank shot by Florida's Bill Lindsay.

Nearly 200 feet away, at the opposite end of the rink, Florida's goalie, John Vanbiesbrouck, faced even more pressure than Patrick. Vanbiesbrouck knew that his team's season would be over if it lost this game in the best-of-seven-games series.

The Avalanche had already beaten the Panthers in the first three games of the championship series. In Game 1, Florida took a 1–0 lead in the first period. The Avalanche rallied with three goals in the second period to win, 3–1. Patrick had made 25 saves in that game. Two nights later, the Avalanche scored four goals in the opening period, including a **hat trick** by Forsberg. Colorado added three goals in the second period and still another in the final period to swamp Florida, 8–1, in the second game. "It was an easy night," Patrick told his friend, professional golfer Fred Couples, after the game. "I saw almost every shot out there tonight."

In Florida for Game 3, the Panthers built a shaky 2–1 lead in the first period, but Patrick stopped the Panthers' last 16 shots over the final 40 minutes. Colorado shooters beat Vanbiesbrouck twice early in the second period to take the lead. The teams played scoreless hockey for the final 37 minutes of regulation, and the Avalanche won, 3–2.

More than 14,700 Panthers fans packed Miami Arena for Game 4. From the start, both teams hustled and scrambled to shoot at the goals. The skaters fired 19 shots at Patrick and Vanbiesbrouck, but the first period ended in a scoreless deadlock. In the second period, the teams combined for 27 shots, but the goalies turned away every puck. Colorado outshot Florida 10–8 in the third period but the buzzer sounded with the score still 0–0. The teams would play a sudden-death overtime period. The first team to score would win.

Three years earlier, the Montreal Canadiens had won 10 straight sudden-death overtime games. The man in goal for Montreal that spring had been Patrick Roy.

Heading into the first extra period, most fans, except Florida fans, felt that Colorado had the edge. The Avalanche outshot Florida 11–7 in the first overtime, but could not put the puck past Vanbiesbrouck. The Panthers could not get a shot past Patrick either. Once, Florida's Rob Niedermayer flew down the right side of the ice with the puck. He eluded the Avalanche defenders and broke in on Patrick. But Patrick stood firm and swatted away Niedermayer's shot.

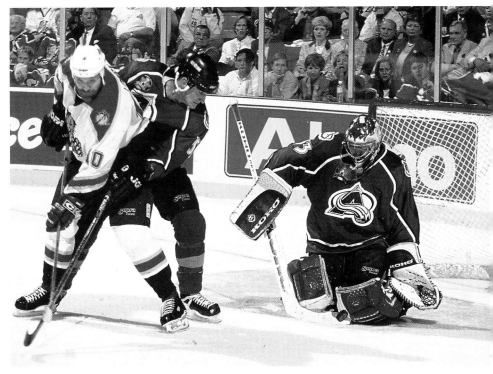

Patrick's stick save stops another Panther shot.

Patrick does a deck save to keep Florida from scoring.

The teams then battled through a second overtime. The Panthers launched 18 shots at Patrick, the most shots by either team in any period of the series. Patrick, with his aggressive style, stopped them all. Colorado took a dozen shots at Vanbiesbrouck, but could not score either.

As the players prepared for the third overtime, long-time hockey fans recalled the longest playoff games ever staged. On March 24, 1936, Detroit's Mud Bruneteau scored 16 minutes and 30 seconds into the sixth overtime period—the ninth period of the game!—to give the Detroit Red Wings a 1–0 victory over the Montreal Maroons in their semifinal series. That is the longest playoff game ever played, but not by much. Three years earlier, in 1933, the Toronto Maple Leafs and Boston Bruins went scoreless 15 minutes and 15 seconds into the sixth overtime period before Ken Doraty won it for the Leafs. In the early rounds of the 1996 playoffs, Petr Nedved of the Pittsburgh Penguins scored with just 45 seconds left in the fourth overtime to beat the Washington Capitals 4–3 in Game 4 of their division semifinal series.

Back and forth, the Avalanche and the Panthers skated as the sixth period began. Both teams had chances, taking three shots each. Then, with the Avalanche on the attack, the puck skittered to the **blue line** where Krupp was stationed at the **left point.** Krupp had missed most of the season with a knee injury, but he was back strong. The lanky defender, who is 6 feet 6 inches tall, wound up and fired the puck. The frozen rubber disk screamed through a maze of players in front of the Panthers' goal and found a tiny opening. The net behind Vanbiesbrouck rippled slightly, and the red light behind the Florida goal flashed. On the scoreboard, which showed the time of the goal as 4:31 of triple overtime, the zero changed to a 1 on Colorado's side.

Vanbiesbrouck hunched over in his **crease** in disappointment. At the other end of the rink, Patrick leaped and raced to join his teammates in celebration. In more than 104 minutes of action, he had faced 63 shots and stopped every one. When the Avalanche had needed him to be perfect, he'd been perfect. In 22 playoff games, he had won 16 times and allowed an average of just 2.10 goals per game. Patrick had added three shutouts to his career playoff stats, bringing that number to 11.

"It was a great game," Patrick said afterward. "John [Vanbiesbrouck] played outstanding. I just tried to keep making good saves."

Patrick had experienced the highest and lowest moments of his career during the season that had just ended. He could only shake his head and marvel at the result of his team's efforts. "There's so much talent on this team," he said. "You have to give [general manager] Pierre Lacroix a lot of credit for the trades he made."

One of the biggest trades, the one that many fans think was the key to Colorado winning the title, was the trade back in December 1995 that moved Patrick to Denver. The Canadian native had never dreamed he would win the Stanley Cup with an American team.

The heavy pads didn't stop Patrick from wanting to play goalie on his youth hockey team.

2

Who's Too Small to Play Goalie?

For Quebec City hockey fans, Colorado's 1996 Stanley Cup title was bittersweet. After all, the Quebec Nordiques had been their team before leaving the mostly French province of Quebec for Denver. The blockbuster trade that sent Patrick Roy from Montreal to Colorado never would have happened if the team had still been playing in Quebec City. The Canadiens and Nordiques had a fierce rivalry. A player as good as Patrick would never have been traded to one rival from the other. But once the Nordiques were sold and moved to Colorado, such restrictions were removed.

Quebec fans did have one reason to be cheerful. After all, Patrick was a local hero. Patrick had been born on October 5, 1965, in Quebec City, Quebec. He was born on the same day another future NHL superstar—Mario Lemieux—was born in Montreal, 160 miles south along the St. Lawrence River.

As a youngster, Patrick was an ardent fan of the Nordiques. Most of the rest of his family was, too, but not his grandmother, Anna Peacock. She cheered for the Montreal Canadiens. She lived with Patrick and his family and took care of the children while their mother, Barbara, coached a swim team. Patrick's father was a successful executive on the Quebec Automobile Insurance Board. Patrick got his first taste of goaltending while playing ball hockey at his home in suburban Ste-Foy, Quebec, with his younger brother, Stephane (STEF-anh).

"We used to play in the house," Patrick recalls. "To make goalie pads, we tied pillows around our legs with belts. We played upstairs with a tennis ball. There was a door at one end of the hallway. That was the goal. We'd shoot balls and try to score on each other. It was fun. Believe it or not, my parents never complained."

When he was six years old, Patrick got his first pair of ice skates. He began to play organized hockey on the frozen rinks of his hometown, slipping and sliding in the outdoor leagues established for kids his age. Although he later became known for his extraordinary ability to stop the puck, Patrick began his hockey career as a **forward.** He soon got his chance to play in the goal cage.

"One day, our goaltender got hit in the leg with the puck," Patrick remembers. "He started crying and said he didn't want to play goalie any more. I said I wanted to be the goalie, but our coach said I was too small."

The following winter, Patrick asked again to play in the goaltender's pads, and this time his coach agreed. "I loved wearing goalie pads," Patrick said. "Even though they were heavy, I thought they were cool."

As a youngster, Patrick cheered for a fellow Quebec native, Atlanta Flames goalie Daniel Bouchard (boo-SHARD). A friend's mother arranged for Patrick to meet Bouchard, and the goaltender gave Patrick a goalie stick he had autographed. Patrick slept with that stick by his bed. In 1978–79, Bouchard led the NHL with 32 victories. Then, halfway through the 1980–81 season, the Flames traded him to Quebec.

"My favorite goaltender was Daniel Bouchard," Patrick admits. "I liked his style so much, I tried to copy it. To stop a shot from the sides, Daniel stood straight up so that he could block the corner of the net. But when he faced shots from the front, he dropped to his knees. His feet stuck straight out on each side to block the bottom of the net."

This technique—known as the "butterfly"—was first made popular by Chicago Blackhawks goaltender Tony Esposito, who is in the hockey Hall of Fame. Bouchard also had tremendous success with the butterfly, winning 286 games in his career.

"I try to play the way Daniel did," says Patrick, "but I sometimes skate farther out of the net than he did.

Daniel Bouchard was Patrick's favorite goaltender.

I try to force guys to get rid of the puck sooner. Hockey players are faster than ever. If you give them an extra second to shoot, they have a better chance to score. If a guy has to make a shot under pressure, he'll usually fire it as hard as he can. Most of the time, the puck goes low. When I'm in the butterfly position, it bounces off my pads or skates. That's why the butterfly is so important to my game."

When Patrick was just 15 years old, he was invited to try out for the Granby Bisons of the Quebec Major Junior Hockey League (QMJHL). The league is an important stepping-stone to the NHL for many Canadian players. Patrick wasn't quite good enough for the team that year, and he was cut. But the following season, when Patrick was 16, he played in 54 games. He won just 13 games and gave up an average of 6.26 goals per game.

"It was tough playing for them," he admitted. "But I got a lot of work and it was a good experience. I learned to deal with the frustrations of losing and I appreciate more the enjoyment of winning."

The Bisons tried to compete but their roster was short on talent. Then, for the 1983–84 season, the Bisons added a forward with a huge **slap shot.** Stephane Richer (REE-shay) scored 39 goals and was the league's top rookie. The team improved, and Patrick's record did too, to 29–29–1. He also brought his **goals-against average** down to 4.44.

This photo shows Patrick doing the butterfly.

Patrick's juniors team, the Granby Bisons, didn't win often.

Each spring, the National Hockey League teams draft young players who have graduated from high school or who are playing in college or the junior leagues. The teams take turns choosing players. Usually, the players are sent to minor league teams to improve before they play with the NHL teams. In the 1984 draft, the Montreal Canadiens used their fourth pick to select Patrick (51st overall) from Granby.

Patrick wasn't quite ready for prime time. Instead, he went back to his juniors team for the 1984–85 season. The Bisons struggled and Patrick won only 16 games while averaging 5.55 goals a game. Still, the experts saw his talent and voted him the league's top goalie.

The Canadiens' scouts also liked what they saw.

Even before the regular season was over, the Canadiens sent 19-year-old Patrick to their American Hockey League (AHL) team in Sherbrooke, Quebec, to try minor league hockey. Patrick played in just one game. He allowed four goals but posted a victory.

Patrick also played in an NHL game that year. On February 23, 1985, he played one period for the Canadiens during a 6–4 victory over the Winnipeg Jets. He did not give up a goal and was credited with the win. Then, Patrick went back to Granby.

Once his juniors season ended, Patrick was sent to Sherbrooke to watch the other goaltenders and to learn. Paul Pageau was Sherbrooke's top goalie and Greg Moffet was the backup. But in the spring of 1985, when the AHL playoffs began, Pageau was called away from the team to be with his wife for the birth of their child. Then, after Moffet was sidelined with equipment trouble one night, Patrick took up his position in goal. He played flawlessly. As the postseason continued, neither Pageau nor Moffet could get the starting job back from the sensational rookie. Patrick won 10 of his 13 games and led all playoff goalies with a 2.89 goals-against average.

"Patrick is making the big saves right now and he is our number one goalie," Sherbrooke coach Pierre Creamer said. Patrick never faltered. The team rode Patrick's hot streak and won the Calder Cup as champion of the AHL.

24

Ready for Prime Time

When Patrick joined the Montreal Canadiens in 1985-86, the team already had a pair of good goalies. Steve Penney, a year ahead of Patrick, had also played in the QMJHL. Penney had earned a spot on the NHL All-Rookie Team in 1984–85 when he won 26 games for the Canadiens. Montreal also had Doug Soetaert, who already had nine years of pro experience with the New York Rangers and Winnipeg Jets. But Patrick felt very confident after his AHL playoff performance. He told everyone what he intended to do.

"I want to be a part of [this year's] team," he said. "Last year, it was felt that Steve Penney needed an experienced backup. This year, I don't think that's the case." The Canadiens had planned to watch Patrick in training camp and then send him to their AHL team to play. They thought they could quickly move him up if either Penney or Soetaert was injured. But in the fall, the Canadiens decided that they would begin the season with three goalies. Patrick had played too well to be sent to the minors.

Of course, he still had a lot to learn about the NHL game. Patrick was just 20 years old, and he had some growing up to do. For one thing, Patrick's diet concerned the Canadiens. Tall and lanky, Patrick was living primarily on junk food—just like many other young people. His favorite food was french fries. Some of his French-speaking teammates nicknamed him "Casseau," the French word for the cardboard box french fries come in.

Patrick had some other wacky habits. He soon became better known for his superstitions than for his brilliant goaltending. "After I pick the stick I'll use for the game, I relax and get dressed," Patrick explained. "I always dress from left to right. I tie my left skate before my right skate. I put on my left glove before my right. It's a superstition, but it also helps me concentrate."

Then, before the start of the game itself, he would skate to the blue line. From there, he'd coldly glare at his goal cage and talk, in his way, to the iron goal posts. "I talk to my goal posts," he explains. "The forwards talk to each other. The defense is always close, but the goaltender is alone."

On some nights, Patrick played as if he were alone on the ice. Sometimes he missed shots he should have stopped. Sometimes he challenged the shooter.

Sometimes he didn't. Just like most rookies, Patrick didn't play consistently. He won his first start, against Mario Lemieux and the Pittsburgh Penguins. Then, his next time in goal, the Boston Bruins shelled him, 7–2. *Toronto Star* hockey writer Rex McLeod wrote this about Patrick: "His gaffes are so extraordinary, and so obvious, that he can't even glare at the defensemen, an old goalie's ruse, to shift the blame."

But soon after that disappointment, Patrick shut out the powerful Edmonton Oilers, who featured Wayne Gretzky, Mark Messier, and Jari Kurri, 4–0. Once more, the Canadiens and their fans were awed by Patrick's ability. "That was an important win for the team and it was important for me as well," said Patrick. "It was the first shutout I had in four years. I looked so bad [in a 5–2 loss to Edmonton], that this was good for me, it restored my confidence."

Patrick passed both Penney and Soetaert to become the team's No. 1 goaltender. He played in 47 of the team's 80 regular-season games and had a record of 23–18–3 with a 3.35 goals-against average. Montreal finished seventh overall in the 21-team league, second to rival Quebec in the Adams Division. The Canadiens finished just one point ahead of Boston, and the two teams would face each other in the first round of the playoffs. The teams would play a seven-game series. The first team to win four games would move on to the next round.

The Canadiens entered the 1986 playoff season with 22 Stanley Cups, more than any other team in NHL history. One more Cup and they would have more championships than any other team in professional sports. But Montreal hadn't won a playoff title in seven years, since 1979. Montreal hockey fans thought the season was a failure if the Canadiens didn't win the Stanley Cup.

There is an unwritten rule in hockey, as in all sports, that members of one team should never say bad things about members of another team, especially if they are about to play them in the playoffs. But some of the Bruins forgot this rule. They were quoted in newspaper stories as doubting Montreal's talent, especially its youngest goalie's talent. "I read what they said about me," said Patrick. "I read where they said that our goaltending was a problem. That stimulated me, motivated me to play well." Patrick and the Canadiens swept Boston in four straight games.

In the next round, Montreal faced the Hartford Whalers. Patrick played excellently, keeping his goals-against average at 2.00 or below for much of the series. The Canadiens beat the Whalers 2–1 in the seventh game to advance, and Patrick's teammates praised him. "I haven't seen goaltending like that in 14 years," said veteran Montreal defenseman Larry Robinson.

"The key was that my coach [Jean Perron] had confidence in me that I could do the job," Patrick said before taking on the New York Rangers in the semifinals. Despite increasing pressure from the Montreal fans, Patrick played as if he were unbeatable. Montreal defeated New York in five games to advance to the Stanley Cup finals against the Calgary Flames.

Before the final series, fans and reporters started comparing Patrick to another Montreal goalie who had taken the team all the way to a title as a rookie.

Reporters wanted to know how Patrick, a rookie, was able to foil the NHL veterans during the 1986 playoffs.

Back in 1971, Ken Dryden had left Cornell University, where he was playing college hockey, to play for Montreal. After only six NHL games, Dryden stepped into Montreal's playoff lineup and led the Canadiens to their 17th Stanley Cup.

Despite Patrick's impressive performance, most fans and reporters expected the Calgary Flames to win the final series in 1986. Calgary had a high-powered offense. In Game 1, the Flames fired 30 shots at Patrick and pounded the Canadiens, 5–2.

Trailing 2–0 in Game 2, Montreal rallied to tie the score. Before many fans had returned to their seats for the start of the overtime period, Brian Skrudland, charged the Flames net and scored. His goal, nine seconds into overtime, ended the shortest overtime period in playoff history. The Canadiens blasted four goals in the first period of Game 3 and won, 5–3.

In the fourth game, Montreal's defensive blanket smothered the Flames' high-octane attack. Patrick stopped all 15 shots by the Calgary shooters. But Mike Vernon was just as good in the Calgary goal, kicking aside every shot from the Canadiens. Finally, halfway through the third period, rookie Claude Lemieux scored to give Montreal a 1–0 lead. Patrick held off the Flames and the Canadiens eked out the narrow victory.

Desperate, the Flames cranked 33 shots at Patrick in Game 5, and scored two goals. But the Canadiens answered with 33 shots of their own, and four got past Vernon. Patrick gave up another goal with just 14 seconds to play, but Montreal held on for the 4–3 victory—and the Stanley Cup! In winning 15 of 20 games, Patrick had allowed just 39 goals—an average of 1.92 per game. He won the Conn Smythe Trophy as the Most Valuable Player in the playoffs.

"The guys were great who played in front of me," Patrick insisted. "They supported me a lot. I have to give credit to the defense because they played that kind of hockey. You could have put 20 names in a hat and any one that you took out would be a good choice [for MVP]."

Two years . . . two playoff titles . . . Not bad for a 20-year-old goalie. Did Patrick let it go to his head?

"I'm pretty lucky. I have never lost in a pro play-off," he said with a laugh. "But winning this year does not make a career. I'm going to come back in training camp and be in good shape and prove myself. Some goaltenders play well in their first year and expect things will be easy in their second year, but they forget how much work you have to do in training camp. It's important to work hard. The most important thing is the desire to practice, the desire to win."

Patrick's future looked bright. Still, what about the next year? What could he possibly do to top winning the Stanley Cup and being the playoffs MVP?

Patrick's early success created high expectations for him to live up to in hockey-crazy Montreal.

Proving Ground

One year Patrick was the best goalie in the Quebec juniors league. The next year he won a minor league playoff title. The year after that, he was a Stanley Cup champion in the NHL. Despite this run of success, Patrick still had a lot to prove. He wanted to prove that he could do a good job, night after night, month after month, year after year.

Ken Dryden, former Montreal goaltending superstar, warned the fans that Patrick might struggle. "When you're new, anything you can provide a team is unexpected and special," Dryden said. "So you can get judged as a prodigy, with people overlooking things about you that aren't so great. But eventually the 14-year-old becomes a 17-year-old and then a 26-year-old. You're not looking for the prodigy any more, you're looking for the artist. You have to grow and meet new standards. And the standards for a goalie are not occasional. It's not the spectacular game that's important, but the routine good performances, day after day."

Patrick was willing to work hard. He brought as much enthusiasm to practice sessions as he did to games, and was always looking for ways to improve.

During the off-season, the champion Canadiens also looked for ways to improve. They traded Steve Penney to Winnipeg for goalie Brian Hayward, who would be Patrick's goaltending teammate.

Although Patrick played well, he wasn't perfect. And one January night, he learned just how tough life in the pros can be. After Patrick gave up four goals on 14 shots against Hartford, Montreal coach Jean Perron yanked him from the game. Patrick skated to the bench to boos from the critical Montreal fans.

The Canadiens finished the regular season with 41 wins and the fifth-best record in the league. Hayward (with a 2.81 goals-against average) and Patrick (at 2.93) were the best goaltending pair in the NHL. They won the Jennings Trophy, which goes to the goalies whose team allows the fewest goals. Still, the Canadiens had some problems. The team had been known for tight defensive play, but the Canadiens weren't trying their hardest every night.

"Sometimes we look like we panic a bit when we make a mistake," Patrick said. "I think the guys want to do too much. They want to do everything right.

Although Patrick was talented, he also struggled at times.

When you want to do too much, you have trouble making the easy play."

Despite these problems, the Canadiens swept the Boston Bruins in the first round. The Quebec Nordiques, Montreal's second-round opponent, provided a greater challenge. Patrick and Hayward took turns playing in goal during the seven-game series. The Canadiens finally managed a 5–3 win in the final game to advance to the conference championship series against Philadelphia.

Hayward played in the first three games of the series with the Flyers. But the Canadiens lost two of those games, so Perron put in Patrick for Game 4. Patrick didn't do very well. He was pulled after giving up four goals. The Canadiens lost the game, 6–3, and were down in the series, three games to one.

"Patrick tried his best," Perron said, "but it wasn't enough. You need to be very strong and make the big saves. I thought he could come back and change the momentum, but it didn't work out that way."

Montreal won Game 5, 5–2, in Philadelphia, as Patrick watched from the bench. He was on the bench for Game 6, too, when the tough, gritty Flyers eked out a 4–3 victory to take the Cup.

When the 1987–88 season began, Patrick felt he had even more to prove. Patrick wanted to show the fans that he could be the Canadiens' best goalie in the long 80-game regular season. He also wanted to prove that he could win in the playoffs.

Patrick began the year playing very well. His season took a horrible turn, however, in an October game against the Minnesota North Stars. Patrick used his big goalie stick to hack away at Minnesota forward Warren Babe.

"The guy **cross-checked** me twice," Patrick said. "Things like that happen in the heat of action. That doesn't excuse it. I've never hit anybody like that before. Anyway, it was not as bad as the Hextall thing."

Philadelphia goaltender Ron Hextall had been suspended for eight games for slashing Edmonton's Kent Nilsson during the 1987 Stanley Cup Finals. The NHL's disciplinary officials did not agree with

Patrick. They handed him the same eight-game ban that they had given Hextall. "It's a tough decision," Patrick said, "but I have no choice but to accept it like a man. It's not my nature. I made a mistake and I have to pay for it. It's that simple."

Two weeks later, Patrick returned to action. He was as sharp as ever. In his first game back, he shut out the Chicago Blackhawks, 3–0, stopping 33 shots. More than 17,800 fans gave him several standing ovations in the Canadiens' home rink, the Forum.

"I was ready," Patrick said. "I worked hard and spent a good deal of time on technique. I worked hard on challenging the shooter and moving around in the crease. It helped me a lot in the first game back."

The Canadiens finished the 1987–88 season atop the Adams Division. Their high finish was due partly to the hard work of Patrick and Hayward. The goaltending pair once again led the NHL in goals-against average. Patrick had a 2.90 goals-against average— third best in the NHL behind Washington's Pete Peeters (2.78) and Hayward (2.86). Going into the playoffs, Montreal was the second-ranked team in the league, trailing only Calgary.

Montreal ousted the Hartford Whalers in the first round, but the series went to six games. In the second round, the Canadiens faced Boston. The Canadiens had knocked the Bruins out of the playoffs in each of the previous two years. When Montreal won the first game, 5–2, it looked as though the Canadiens would end the Bruins' season again. But Montreal's scorers went into a slump. Boston's goalies, Reggie Lemelin and Andy Moog, gave up just five goals in the next four games. Patrick made save after save, but he could not carry the team alone. The Canadiens lost the second-round series, four games to one—a huge disappointment.

As the last line of defense, Patrick could never let up.

Nothing was more important to the Canadiens than getting back to the Stanley Cup Finals in the 1988–89 season. Montreal's owners replaced Perron, who had been Patrick's number one fan, with Pat Burns. A tough coach, Burns was known to be demanding but fair. The players responded positively to the change. The Canadiens played more consistently. They became even more difficult to score against than they had been in the previous two years when they led the league with the lowest goals-against average.

Patrick improved too. He brought his goals-against average down and down and down. By season's end, he had his all-time best average, 2.47. "I think it would be a great thing for our team if we could win the Jennings Trophy for the third year in a row," Patrick said. "We have been consistent all season. Game after game, we concentrate well and we have worked hard every night."

Patrick had been thinking about more than hockey during the season. He and his wife, Michele, were building a family, too. On March 15, 1989, Michele gave birth to their first child, Jonathan. That night, Patrick beat the Kings 5–2 to celebrate.

Patrick told one interviewer that, as a goalie, "You don't want to give the other team any hope." The rest of the NHL didn't seem to have any hope of winning at the Forum. The victory over Los Angeles boosted Patrick's home-ice record to 23–0–2. Bill Durnan, a

Montreal legend, had compiled a 22–0–3 record at the Forum in 1933–34. Patrick finished the season with a record of 25–0–3 at home.

Montreal finished the season on top of the Adams Division with 53 wins. Once again, the Canadiens were just behind Calgary in the overall standings. With a team goals-against average of 2.72, Patrick and Hayward won their third Jennings Trophy. With a league-best 2.47 GAA, Patrick won his first Vezina Trophy as the best goalie in the NHL.

Despite the awards, Patrick and all the Canadiens focused on the playoffs. They were determined to meet the challenge of doing better than they had the previous two years.

And they did. Montreal needed only four games to sweep Hartford in the first round, although two of the games went to sudden-death overtime. The Canadiens defeated Boston in five games in the second round. Montreal was playing very well. Next, the Canadiens faced the Philadelphia Flyers. Two years earlier, the Flyers had beaten Montreal in the semifinals. The two teams were back, playing for the right to play in the Stanley Cup Finals.

Patrick was ready but, in Game 1, his teammates clearly weren't. The Flyers broke Patrick's 34-game home unbeaten streak by defeating the Canadiens 3–1. Patrick responded with a 3–0 shutout victory in Game 2. In Game 3, Montreal shelled the Flyers 5–1.

Patrick shows off his Vezina Trophy, along with, from left, his mother, wife, and father.

Then Patrick shut them out again, 3–0, before heading home to the Forum for Game 5.

Patrick and Hextall, Philadelphia's goalie, held the teams to a 1–1 tie in regulation play. Then, the Flyers slapped one past Patrick in overtime to force a sixth game. Montreal's defense was too much for Philadelphia in that game, limiting the Flyers to two goals in a 4–2 series-clinching victory. The Canadiens were back in the Stanley Cup Finals for the first time in three years!

"I'm at my best when I really concentrate," Patrick said. "Sometimes during the long regular season, it's hard to focus on my job. But it's easy to concentrate during the playoffs. The pressure makes me focus, and that usually helps me play better. I don't let any negative things go through my head. I try to think positive thoughts. In my mind, I picture myself making saves before I make them."

Montreal faced a strong Calgary Flames team in the Finals. The Flames had been the top team during the NHL's regular season. After the Canadiens won two of the first three games, Montreal fans were excited and confident. The Canadiens would win it all! Then, Montreal's troubles started. The Canadiens scored just two goals in each of the next three games. Flames goalie Mike Vernon played brilliantly. Patrick finished with a 2.09 goals-against average. Vernon was second at 2.26, but Vernon won the last three games and the Stanley Cup.

Patrick began the 1989-90 season with one aim—to win back the Stanley Cup. He played magnificently, leading the NHL in wins (31), goals-against average (2.53), and **save percentage** (91.2). Patrick earned his second Vezina Trophy as the league's best goalie, but his team didn't do as well. Montreal slipped to third in the Adams Division.

Patrick was particularly sharp in goal as the Canadiens bumped off Buffalo in the first round of playoffs.

"When you have the best goaltender in the league, anything can happen," said Coach Burns. But Boston beat Patrick and the Canadiens in the second round, four games to one. Another season ended in playoff disappointment for Montreal.

Patrick's troubles got worse midway through the 1990–91 season. Patrick was knocked out of the lineup when he hurt his knee. He had missed games before when he was suspended and when he had tonsillitis, but this was the first time he was out with an injury.

Shortly after he returned to action in January, he shut out a strong Buffalo team. But the very next night, in a game against Boston, disaster struck. Patrick left his goal cage to clear a loose puck. A Bruin forward and a Montreal defenseman were tangling around the net. In the scramble, the pair fell on Patrick, who tore ligaments in his left ankle.

While he was healing, his team tried to overcome the loss of an all-star goalie. Meanwhile, Patrick was busy at home. His wife, Michele, gave birth to their second son, Frederick, on February 26, 1991.

By March, Patrick could play again. In his first week back, he stopped a career-high 49 shots in a game against Chicago. His coach said Patrick meant as much to Montreal's team as Wayne Gretzky did to his. "It's always nice to hear that from my coach," Patrick said. "I just try to give some leadership and make the saves that keep the team in the big games."

In mid-March, Patrick's ankle injury flared up. He couldn't play every day. His team was struggling, too. As the playoffs began, Montreal's players, coaches, and fans worried about the Canadiens' chances.

In the first round, Montreal edged Buffalo. Then, for the fourth year in a row, the Canadiens faced Boston in the second round. Two of the games went into overtime before the hard-fought series ended when the Bruins won Game 7, 2–1.

Things didn't start out any better in the 1991–92 season. In just the second week of the new season, Buffalo's Christian Ruuttu (RUH-too) unleashed a hard shot that blasted Patrick in the side of the face. A large bump quickly swelled on Patrick's right jaw. He rushed to the hospital for X-rays, and was relieved to find out that he hadn't broken any bones. Patrick was soon back in uniform. By mid-season, his goals-against average was under 2.00. "I'm having my best season in the NHL," Patrick said. "I'm concentrating better. I think I'm an improved goaltender."

Montreal won its division by a wide margin, finishing with the fifth-best record in the league (41–28–11). Patrick had played in a career-high 67 games and won 36 of his team's victories. He also led the league in shutouts (5) and goals-against average (2.36, his lowest ever). For the third time, he won the Vezina Trophy. He also won a fourth Jennings Trophy, but what he really wanted was another Stanley Cup.

The Boston Bruins were often playoff foes for Montreal.

Montreal barely squeaked past Hartford in the first round. Russ Courtnall scored in the overtime of Game 7 to move Montreal to the second round. The Boston Bruins swept the Canadiens in round two. Patrick and the Canadiens had reached bottom. One reporter harshly described Patrick as "a bumbling shadow of his former self."

That summer, fans heard rumors that Patrick was headed to the Quebec Nordiques in return for Eric Lindros. Lindros had been selected first overall in the 1991 draft but he had refused to play for the Nordiques. He was willing to play for Montreal. But the Canadiens didn't trade Patrick. Instead, they hired Jacques Demers as their coach and began building what they hoped would be a brighter future.

An Angry Good-bye

When several playoff flops followed brilliant regular seasons, Patrick became a target for fierce criticism. Montreal fans were polled in 1992–93 as to whether they thought Patrick should be traded. More than half felt he should be. Patrick had won honor after honor and had even been the MVP when the Canadiens last won the Stanley Cup, but he was blamed for many of Montreal's losses.

Although Patrick was far from perfect and had played poorly at times, he wasn't the only Canadien to blame. The Canadiens had once focused on defense, but lately they had begun to concentrate more on scoring. That meant they didn't give Patrick as much help in guarding the net. Patrick's goals-against average began to swell. He finished the year with 31 wins, but his GAA was 3.20—much higher than the 2.36 that had earned him the Vezina Trophy in 1992.

Adding good scorers, such as Vincent Damphousse, Brian Bellows, Kirk Muller, and Denis Savard had paid off for Montreal. The Canadiens won 48 games and finished with the sixth-best record in the NHL. The playoffs would be their biggest test. If the Canadiens failed, the team would almost certainly be dismantled.

In the first round, Montreal beat Quebec in six grueling games. Montreal lost Game 1 in overtime, but earned overtime victories in Games 3 and 5. The Canadiens' second-round battle with Buffalo was a nail-biter from the first faceoff to the final buzzer. Montreal swept the series in four straight games, winning each game by the score of 4–3. The last three games went into overtime. By the end of the series, Montreal had five straight overtime wins. Patrick was the key in each one.

In the third round, the Canadiens faced the New York Islanders. The Islanders had upset the Stanley Cup champion Pittsburgh Penguins in the second round. Games 2 and 3 went into overtime, but each time, Patrick shut down the Islanders until his teammates found a way to score the game-winner. After five games, Montreal had earned its first trip to the Stanley Cup Finals since 1989. The Canadiens would play Wayne Gretzky and the Los Angeles Kings. Los Angeles was on a roll after eliminating Calgary, Vancouver, and Toronto in the early rounds.

The Canadiens played sluggishly in Game 1. The Kings peppered Patrick with 38 shots and scored an easy 4–1 victory. But Patrick's busy day wasn't over even after the game. Hours after the Canadiens had lost, Patrick went to the hospital with his wife. The next morning, their daughter, Jana, was born.

Although Patrick hadn't gotten a lot of rest the previous night, he and the Canadiens were determined to even the series in Game 2. Montreal trailed 2–1 late in the game. Then, Kings defenseman Marty McSorley was penalized for using an illegal stick. On the **power play,** Montreal defenseman Eric Desjardins (DAY-zhar-dan) scored his second goal of the game to tie the score, 2–2, and send the game into overtime.

Patrick had seven overtime wins already to his credit in the playoffs. He was ready. But he didn't even have to make a save. Teammate Desjardins cranked the winning goal past Kelly Hrudey 51 seconds into overtime.

Two nights later, in Los Angeles, Montreal had a 3–0 lead but the Kings rallied for a 3–3 tie after 60 minutes. This time, John LeClair poked the winning goal past Hrudey 34 seconds into the overtime.

The Kings just wouldn't quit. They cranked 42 shots at Patrick in Game 4. The Kings tied the game at 2–2 to force a sudden-death overtime period for the third straight game. In the last two overtimes, Patrick had faced just one shot! This overtime period was different. The teams skated back and forth for nearly 15 minutes, trading shots. Ten times the Kings fired at Patrick, but he turned away each shot. Finally, at 14:37 of the extra period, LeClair skated in the slot area and banged a loose puck past Hrudey. Montreal was one victory away from its 24th Stanley Cup!

"We didn't mind going into overtime," Patrick said. "I knew my teammates were going to score goals if I gave them some time. My concentration was at such a high level. I felt fresh, like I could stop everything."

Back at the Forum for Game 5, the Canadiens scored twice late in the second period to turn a 1–1 nail-biter into a 4–1 trouncing. Patrick stopped 18 shots. He raised his second Stanley Cup and also won the playoff MVP trophy for the second time.

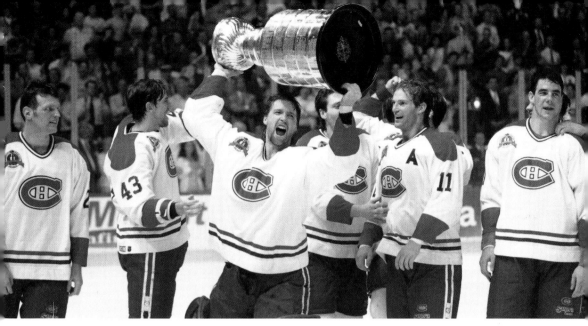
Holding the Stanley Cup, Patrick celebrates the victory.

With a playoff record of 16–4 and a goals-against average of 2.13, Patrick had silenced the critics who, earlier in the year, had called for him to be traded. The Canadiens rewarded their goalie with a four-year contract worth at least $16 million, plus bonuses.

In the 1993–94 season, Patrick played in a career-high 68 games and led the league with seven shutouts. He had a brilliant 2.50 goals-against average. The Canadiens faced their rivals from Boston in the first round of the playoffs.

The Canadiens lost Game 1, 3–2, but they came back to win Game 2 by the same score. Their excitement at evening the series was dampened, however. After the game, Patrick went to the hospital. He had appendicitis, a serious infection.

Pierre Lacroix, a friend of Patrick's, visited him in the hospital. "He was laying there, all hooked up to tubes and wires, tears in his eyes, telling me how much he wanted to play," Lacroix recalled. "I stopped and bought him a computer golf game. We started playing. We get to the 17th hole. I'm up by two strokes. It's a par-3, 220-yard hole. Patrick selects his 3-wood and makes a hole in one. Well, he lets out a scream like you can't believe and he just keeps on screaming. The guard came rushing in. Everyone thought we were fighting or Patrick was dying. We're laughing and there are tears rolling down our faces."

Patrick missed Game 3, which the Canadiens lost. But after three days of taking antibiotics in the hospital, Patrick decided he felt better and could play. He checked himself out of the hospital and returned to the team for Game 4. Patrick stopped 39 shots for a 5–2 victory. He played his finest hockey in the third period when he shut down the Bruins even though they took 15 shots at him. Patrick's phenomenal play continued in Game 5 when he made 60 saves, including 16 in overtime. With the 2–1 overtime victory, Montreal led the series, three games to two. But the Canadiens lost the next two games and the series. Four days after Game 7, Patrick went back to the hospital and doctors removed his infected appendix.

The 1994–95 season didn't start out well for Patrick or any NHL player. The team owners and players couldn't agree on how much money the players should earn. The two sides argued and argued, delaying the start of the season for nearly three months until they agreed on a new contract.

The Canadiens' troubles didn't end with the start of the season. They didn't play well. Patrick thought the problem was a lack of effort. One night, in the locker room between periods of a game against the Flyers, Patrick criticized the play of Montreal defenseman Mathieu Schneider. The two got into a brief fist fight. Not long after the scuffle, Schneider was traded.

The Canadiens finished with the 10th-worst record in the league. For the first time in 25 years, Montreal would not be in the playoffs.

"People demand the Stanley Cup every year, but it's not realistic," Patrick said. "I could never believe that the Canadiens would one day miss the playoffs. But we were so bad on the road [3–18–3] that you can't expect to make the playoffs. Maybe we're not as good as people think. It's the first time since juniors that I've been through this. It's a new experience and I hope I'll gain from it."

Following their 18–23–7 finish in the shortened 48-game season, the Canadiens fired General Manager Serge Savard and hired former Montreal winger Rejean Houle to take his place. They also dismissed Coach Jacques Demers and replaced him with Mario Tremblay, another former player.

Patrick showed up for work in the fall of 1995 ready to prove himself all over again. "My objective," he announced, "is to play as much as possible and be consistent. Last year was a roller coaster. I had some good games, but some shaky ones, too."

Even with his renewed dedication to stopping the puck, Patrick struggled. On opening night, he gave up five goals on 22 shots before Tremblay pulled him from the game in the second period. The Canadiens lost, 7–1—the team's worst season-opening loss ever.

Things only got worse. When the team didn't play well, Coach Tremblay boiled over and blasted his players. He criticized Patrick, too. The locker room was full of angry, unhappy players.

On December 2, 1995, the Detroit Red Wings came to the Forum for a game that ESPN would televise across the United States and Canada. Just three minutes into the game, Patrick gave up a goal on a power play. Five minutes later, Slava Kozlov fooled Patrick and gave Detroit a 2–0 lead. Before the first period ended, Kozlov had scored again, as had Nicklas Lidstrom and Greg Johnson. When the period ended, Detroit led, 5–1.

Normally, a team that is behind by that much after one period will replace its goalie during the break. But Coach Tremblay left Patrick in for the second period. And Detroit kept firing away. Within the first five minutes of the middle session, the Red Wings extended their lead to 7–1.

Once during the flurry Patrick made a routine save. The Forum crowd cheered sarcastically and Patrick raised his arms in mock celebration. Midway through the period, Johnson scored again, followed quickly by Sergei Fedorov. Detroit led 9–1 with nearly half the game remaining.

Coach Tremblay finally sent backup goalie Pat Jablonski in for Patrick. Patrick was angry. He thought his coach had left him in the game just to embarrass him. His teammates hadn't been playing very well either. Patrick thought that as the number one goalie, he shouldn't have to play when he was having a bad night. On his way to the end of the bench, Patrick glared at his coach. Then Patrick went to the box seat behind the team bench and spoke to Canadiens president Ronald Corey.

"This is my last game in Montreal," Patrick told him. Then Patrick screamed at Coach Tremblay, "Did you understand?" He slumped at the end of the bench.

"Was Patrick embarrassed? I'm sure he was," Coach Tremblay said later. "I didn't purposely leave him in the game to antagonize him. I'm not the kind of guy who would do that to an athlete. But I'm not here for players to like me. I'm here to win hockey games."

The next morning, Patrick skipped practice and a team meeting. Coach Tremblay suspended him. About 48 hours later, Patrick and teammate Mike Keane had been traded to Colorado. In return, Montreal got goaltender Jocelyn Thibault (TEE-boh) and forwards Andrei Kovalenko and Martin Rucinsky.

Two months later, the Canadiens went to McNichols Sports Arena in Denver to play the Avalanche. Before the game, Patrick offered $3,000 to his new teammates for a team party if they won the game. They did, 4–2. After the game, in which he made 37 saves, Patrick flipped the game puck at Tremblay as he walked off the ice.

Fighting back tears, Patrick says good-bye to Montreal hockey fans after being traded to Colorado.

Late in April 1996, the Avalanche began its playoff roll. The Colorado players flattened Vancouver, Chicago, and Detroit to get to the Stanley Cup Finals. After Patrick had won 12 of the 18 playoffs games, a reporter asked him why he was playing so well. Patrick said his father had given him a few tips. The reporter asked what those tips were. "Can you keep a secret," asked Patrick. The reporter said he could. "So can I," Patrick said, smiling and walking away.

Colorado had to fight off a stiff challenge from the Florida Panthers to win the Stanley Cup. Many Avalanche players played well in that series, but none were better than the man the Colorado fans call "Saint Patrick," king of goalies.

"I always dreamed of winning the Stanley Cup," Patrick said. "After I had won it once, I started dreaming of winning it again and again. A lot of people think I'm cocky. I don't think I'm cocky. I just believe in myself, and I'll do anything to win."

In the 1997 playoffs, Colorado defeated Chicago and Edmonton in the first two rounds. Detroit—the eventual Stanley Cup champion—stopped the Avalanche in the semifinals.

Patrick made NHL playoff history by passing Billy Smith in career playoff wins. (Smith had 88 postseason wins for the four-time Stanley Cup champion New York Islanders.) But to Patrick, that honor was small consolation for his team losing.

"I'm not afraid to look in the mirror when it's not going well," he said. "In Montreal, I was hard on some guys, but not as hard as I am on myself. I can't accept lack of effort, although I'm learning it's part of the game. In Colorado, I don't have to worry about saying anything. We have a coach [Marc Crawford] who is the same as me—he won't accept lack of effort.

"I've made some mistakes," he continued, "but, hey, nobody's perfect. You learn from your mistakes. For me the will to win is what it's all about. That's it. There's nothing else."

Career Highlights

Regular Season Statistics

Minor Leagues	Team	W–L–T	Games	Minutes	GA	GAA
1982–83	Granby (QMJHL)	13–35–1	54	2,808	293	6.26
1983–84	Granby (QMJHL)	29–29–1	61	3,585	265	4.44
1984–85	Granby (QMJHL)	16–25–1	44	2,463	228	5.55
	Sherbrooke (AHL)	1–0–0	1	60	4	4.00
Totals		59–89–3	160	8,916	790	5.32
NHL						
1984–85	Montreal	1–0–0	1	20	0	0.00
1985–86	Montreal	23–18–3	47	2,651	148	3.35
1986–87	Montreal	22–16–6	46	2,686	131	2.93
1987–88	Montreal	23–12–9	45	2,586	125	2.90
1988–89	Montreal	33–5–6	48	2,744	113	2.47
1989–90	Montreal	31–16–5	54	3,173	134	2.53
1990–91	Montreal	25–15–6	48	2,835	128	2.71
1991–92	Montreal	36–22–8	67	3,935	155	2.36
1992–93	Montreal	31–25–5	62	3,595	192	3.20
1993–94	Montreal	35–17–11	68	3,867	161	2.50
1994–95	Montreal	17–20–6	43	2,566	127	2.97
1995–96	Montreal	12–9–1	22	1,260	62	2.95
	Colorado	22–15–1	39	2,305	103	2.68
1996–97	Colorado	38–15–7	62	3,697	143	2.32
	Totals	349–205–74	652	37,920	1,722	2.72

GA = goals allowed.   GAA = goals against average.

Playoff Statistics

Minor Leagues	Team	W–L–T	Games	Minutes	GA	GAA
1983–84	Granby (QMJHL)	0–4	4	244	22	5.41
1984–85	Granby (QMJHL)	—	—	—	—	—
	Sherbrooke (AHL)	10–3	13	769	37	2.89
Totals		10–7	17	1,013	59	3.49
NHL						
1984–85	Montreal	—	—	—	—	—
1985–86	Montreal	15–5	20	1,218	39	1.92
1986–87	Montreal	4–2	6	330	22	4.00
1987–88	Montreal	3–4	8	430	24	3.35
1988–89	Montreal	13–6	19	1,206	42	2.09
1989–90	Montreal	5–6	11	641	26	2.43
1990–91	Montreal	7–5	13	785	40	3.06
1991–92	Montreal	4–7	11	686	30	2.62
1992–93	Montreal	16–4	20	1,293	46	2.13
1993–94	Montreal	3–3	6	375	16	2.56
1994–95	Montreal	—	—	—	—	—
1995–96	Colorado	16–6	22	1,454	51	2.10
1996–97	Colorado	10–7	17	1,033	38	2.21
Totals		96–55	153	9,451	374	2.37

Glossary

blue line: One of two 12-inch-wide blue lines on the ice that mark where a team's defensive zone begins. A blue line is 60 feet in front of a goal.

crease: A semicircle with a 6-foot radius or a rectangle in front of the goal. Players can't be in the other team's crease unless the puck is there.

cross-checked: Hit by the stick of another player when that player is holding it with both hands, unless part of the stick is on the ice.

defenseman: A player who helps the goaltender protect their team's goal. A team has two defensemen out on the ice at a time.

forward: A player whose primary responsibility is to score. A team has three forwards on the ice. The forward in the middle is the *center*. The other forwards are the *left wing* and the *right wing*.

goals-against average (GAA): The average number of goals a goaltender allows for each minute he or she is on the ice. Goals scored into an empty net after the goaltender has been pulled for an extra attacker are not counted. To figure a goalie's goals-against average, multiply the number of goals the goalie has given up by 60 (the number of minutes in a regulation game). Then divide that number by the number of minutes the goalie was in the game. For example, let's say Patrick has allowed 21 goals in 7 games and he has played every minute of six of those games and two periods of the seventh game. (Each period is 20 minutes, or 0.33 of a game.) He has played 6.66 x 60, or 399.6 minutes. To figure his GAA, we would do this: $21 \times 60 = 1{,}260$. 1,260 divided by 399.6 = 3.15.

hat trick: The scoring of three or more goals by the same person in one game.

left point: An imaginary point to the left of the goal just inside the blue line. The defensemen are often positioned at the left and right points.

power play: The offense used when one team has more players on the ice because the other team has one or more players in the penalty box.

save percentage: The percentage of saves a goaltender makes in each game. To figure a goalie's save percentage, divide the total number of saves the goalie has made by the total number of shots (saves and goals) he or she has faced. For example, if Patrick has made 28 saves and allowed 2 goals, 28 divided by 30 = 0.933. Move the decimal point two places to the right for his save percentage, 93.3%.

slap shot: A shot in which the shooter draws back the stick to shoulder height before swinging and hitting the puck.

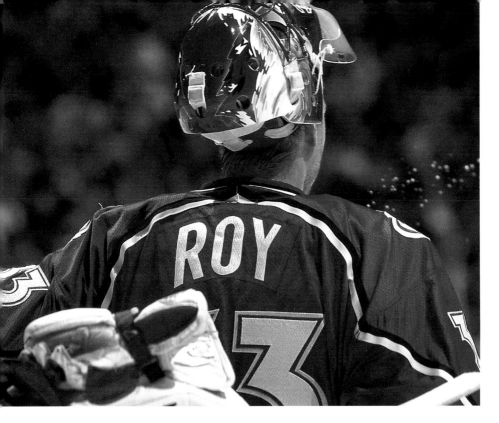

Sources

Information for this book was obtained from the following sources: Jerry Crasnick (*Sports Illustrated for Kids*, May 1997); Helene Elliott (*The Los Angeles Times*, 11 June 1996); Michael Farber (*Sports Illustrated*, 18 December 1995); Douglas Hunter (*A Breed Apart, An Illustrated History of Goaltending*, 1995); Joe LaPointe (*The New York Times*, 11 June 1996); E. M. Swift (*Sports Illustrated*, 21 June 1993); Larry Wigge, (*The Sporting News*, 17 June 1996); *The Complete Encyclopedia of Hockey*, 4th edition (1993); *The National Hockey League Official Guide and Record Book 1996–97; The National Hockey League 1996 Stanley Cup Playoffs Fact Guide.*

Index

Write to Patrick:

You can send mail to Patrick at the address on the right. If you write a letter, don't get your hopes up too high. Patrick and other athletes get lots of letters every day, and they aren't always able to answer them all.

Patrick Roy
c/o The Colorado Avalanche
McNichols Sports Arena
Denver, CO 80204

ıll....ıll..ıllıllıılllıııtıılı..ıtılıtİıtlıtı

Acknowledgments

Photographs reproduced with permission from: p. 1, SportsChrome East/West, Rob Tringali, Jr.; pp. 2, 3, 12, © ALLSPORT USA/Al Bello; p. 6, Robert Laberge, CHC; p. 9, Archive Photos/Gary C. Caskey/Reuters; p. 11, © ALLSPORT USA/Rick Stewart; p. 15, © ALLSPORT USA/Glenn Cratty; pp. 16, 22, Courtesy of La Voix de l'Est; p. 20 (top), Hockey Hall of Fame; pp. 20 (bottom), 54, Sports-Chrome East/West, Craig Melvin; pp. 24, 29, 32, 35, 38, 41, Bob Fisher, CHC; pp. 45, 46, 51, André Pichette, CHC; p. 49, Archive Photos/Gary Hershorn/Reuters; p. 57, Archive Photos/Shaun Best/Reuters; p. 62, SportsChrome East/West, Scott Brinegar.

Front cover photograph by © ALLSPORT USA/Nevin Reid. Back cover photograph by © ALLSPORT USA. Artwork by Sean Todd.

About the Author

Morgan Hughes is the author of two other sports biographies for young readers. A freelance writer, Morgan lives with his family in Pennsylvania.